Raising ADHD Teenage Girls

How to Manage ADHD Habits and Emotions in Girls

Elizabeth Braun

Contents

INTRODUCTION

I'm a 42-year old housewife and mother of a beautiful 15-year-old girl. Early in life, she showed signs of ADHD disorder. Her childhood years weren't always straightforward, but they were full of blissful moments I treasure. I wrote this book to share my experiences with other parents of children with ADHD or parents whose children have recently been diagnosed.

When doctors first diagnosed my daughter, negative and depressive thoughts consumed me. I didn't understand what it all meant. I didn't want to understand. I wanted to reject it. Over time though, with the doctor's advice, other parents' stories, and my experiences, I developed a framework that helped us both.

This allowed me to enjoy her childhood, as I do to this day. ADHD can be managed so that children have relatively everyday and successful lives. It's about managing the specifics, unique to every child, that need to be considered. By doing this, signs of ADHD can be masked well to fit capably into society.

This book sheds light on our experiences, lessons learned from her early years into the present day. Dealing with teenagers isn't easy, and ADHD doesn't make things simpler. As my daughter's hormones kicked in, she started lapsing in self-control I'd built up in her about consistently taking her ADHD medications. On top of that, she often attributed social and physical problems to her disorder, which quickly led to her feeling alone and depressed. It's hard to make a teenager listen to an adult's advice, and it's next to impossible for teenagers with ADHD.

The good news is that if you've worked alongside your child's illness for so long, it's easier to work with and adapt to as they go through changes in their lives. This is my journey, and personal experiences that helped my daughter and I adjust and lead regular social lives. We're all different, and our situations may not be similar to yours.

But in writing this book, I hope something we did can be of use to you if you're in a similar position. It's not a book offering medical advice but a personal story of triumph against all odds.

Part I

Just Getting Started

Chapter 1: What Experts Say about ADHD

When I started to suspect my daughter may have ADHD, I busied my time reading as much as I could. From books to endless internet research, I consumed every bit of information I could. I'm not a doctor or scientist, but I tried to learn as much as possible, even if some of the information was hearsay. My investigations led me to the following conclusions.

ADHD is a disorder attributed to psychiatric, neurologic, and genetic malfunctions. The abbreviation stands for "attention deficit hyperactivity disorder". It can manifest itself in various ways, the most common being ADD (attention deficit disorder).

A scientific article on the history of ADHD, "The history of attention deficit hyperactivity disorder," says the first time ADHD was documented in 1798 by a Scottish physician, Alexander Crichton. Many years afterward, it was also recorded and diagnosed in children by other researchers, namely the British pediatrician Sir George Still. In 1902, he wrote about the abnormal moral control deficiency in children. During the 20th century, psychiatric and neurological diagnostics revealed more ADHD cases. Then in the early 2000s, the American Academy of Pediatrics formulated the clinical symptoms of ADHD. And today, these remain predominantly unchanged. The most recent version can be viewed on the AAP website.

ADHD is usually attributed to the genetic abnormalities that result in the malfunctioning of a particular part of the human brain. While a range of results was discovered through many studies, most noted was that a developmental issue in the frontal lobes of a child's brain seemed to be the instigating factor for ADHD.

The frontal lobe controls impulse activity, memory, problem-solving, decision making, and other essential processes. At correlating ages, children with ADHD had smaller frontal lobes. Most research concluded that the number and activity of neurotransmitters were different in these children's brains. That meant information passed on from the frontal lobes was either weaker or wired incorrectly than children without ADHD. Much of it is still a mystery, though. The possible neurotransmitters responsible for ADHD could be dopamine and norepinephrine.

The Academy for Psychiatry says ADHD can manifest less acutely in a child while growing. This is linked to the growth and maturity of the brain. In adults, having a fully developed brain, ADHD might only be evident on stressful occasions.

ADHD has multiple symptoms. A child with ADHD doesn't necessarily manifest all symptoms. Some may be accentuated, some less so. These are two main ones that are evident in most cases:

- Lack of attention and an inability to focus on something for long periods.

- Hyperactivity and impulsiveness. Constant motion, often chaotic, an inability to "slow down" and quieten after being excited.

- Here are some other possible symptoms:

- An inability to sit still. Twisting around and often standing up and moving around.

- Poor self-control when talking and constantly interrupting other people when speaking.

- A short concentration period relevant to their age compared to children without ADHD.

- An inability to follow instructions if there is more than one topic to be followed (this can develop with age).

- Frequent falls and bumps; somewhat careless in motion; and an inadequate danger evaluation (in some kids, there seems to be no safety instinct at all).

- Often losing personal objects and forgetting things and appointments.

- Difficulty changing their focus when asked.

By 2020, AAP guidelines stated that ADHD can be diagnosed in 4-year old children. Still, with most kids, the diagnosis is established or suspected at the start of their school years. According to the Center for Disease Control, the non-consistent presence of ADHD symptoms under four cannot be the ground for a diagnosis. Six signs need to be prevalent, constantly, for at least six months for a doctor to diagnose. The criteria are slightly different (minimum 5 symptoms) if they vary in intensity.

Depending on the present symptoms, ADHD can be divided into three presentations:

- Mainly inattentive (shows a lack of attentiveness, minor hyperactivity symptoms).

- Predominantly hyperactive (the child can concentrate on the task but displays excessive motion and fidgeting).

- Combined (both main symptoms of ADHD are represented).

In the US psychiatric practice, ADHD treatment includes behavioral therapy, education counseling, and medication. The medication (mostly psychostimulants, amphetamines, and methylphenidates) aims to relieve the symptoms. The Sydney Cognitive Center states it provides a temporary effect, and side effects should be considered. In addition to medication, a complex treatment including social and behavioral aspects is necessary.

Another opinion on ADHD is that it's nothing more than a "marketing diagnosis". This take on ADHD considers the child's behavior as a variable norm, and no special treatment is required. As a parent of an ADHD child, I'd say it's pretty tempting to take this point of view for granted. Although a child with ADHD shouldn't be treated as a "sick" kid. This concept, however, provides no assistance for parents in combating the road ahead. And that road entails making a child's day less chaotic, helping them concentrate, having fewer accidents, losing fewer things such as pens, toys, and clothes.

For me, the traditional understanding of ADHD described by the AAP felt like a more sound option with established guidelines I believed would help us. The treatment can always be discussed in length with your doctor, and make sure all medical terms are understood. Listen, and ask again and again until you fully understand. Don't be afraid to question prescriptions and ask about side effects and desirable results. Cooperate and be open about your doubts and concerns. There's a long road ahead, and you want your doctor to be on the same page as you.

Chapter 2: Understanding ADHD in Girls

The CDC data shows that boys are diagnosed with ADHD three times more often than girls. However, the experts say this disparity appears due to so many children going undiagnosed, so it's not a true reflection on numbers.

The combined and hypersensitive types of ADHD are less frequent in girls. It's more likely for a girl to have ADD. The latter has fewer external symptoms and can often be overlooked at the toddler and preschool age.

Typical ADD symptoms in girls include the following:

- Daydreaming, not "being present". This can manifest itself as a stable condition or appear during conversations, lessons, etc.

- Anxiety. A girl with ADHD or ADD might be less active than a boy with the same diagnosis but display more mental problems. With some girls, this can lead to eating disorders as well.

- Inability to focus on a task.

- Memory gaps, a girl often cannot find the words to express herself correctly.

- Low academic performance.

- Low confidence and self-esteem.

Girls with ADD or ADHD are often considered "quiet" and "daydreamers". They also tend to subconsciously hide their disorder until the first academic achievement grades are received. Girls with ADHD tend to direct their emotions internally, making them appear less impulsive.

Over the years, the suppressed symptoms of ADHD in girls might lead to the following behavioral patterns:

- Frequent depressive states without an apparent reason

- High-stress level during routine tasks

- Low self-esteem and self-comparison with other girls

- Obsessive movements (nail-biting, constantly touching their clothes or parts of the body, etc.)

- The predominance of emotions during decision making

- Sudden bursts of emotions such as tears or bursts of laughter

- Failing to grasp a response vs. consequence scenario

Cultural patterns can also influence the underdiagnosis of ADHD in girls. If a girl is perceived as quiet and shy, this demure behavior may be accepted and encouraged. People may believe there is nothing wrong with her. Sadly, her lack of concentration will be frowned upon in academics. This could lead to her feeling detached and withdrawing further from society as low self-esteem takes over.

Have you noticed that your daughter has difficulty concentrating on a task for a specific time (it can be 5-10 minutes for 4-year old kids)? Does she often lose the trail of a conversation? Does she interrupt you people talking to her all the time in mid-sentence? Does she seem distracted and in her own world more than necessary? Is she forever losing things? ADHD might be the reason for this behavior.

However, avoid being extreme in the analyzing process as you don't want to envision ADHD symptoms in every movement and action your child makes. Behavior can also be affected by personal situations, such as family trauma, divorce, etc.

The main attribute of ADHD is its consistency. It doesn't disappear as they age. The symptoms may also change as the child grows. Therefore, if your child may appear distracted and overly emotional one day and composed the next, chances are, they do not suffer from ADHD.

Reading about ADHD in girls, parents often wrongly perceive this illness as dull and gloomy. As though a child must sit in solitary confinement and not interact with the environment around them. This is far from the truth, and children with ADHD can be joyous and active. You'll probably notice though they're often falling, bumping into other children. It can be sudden excitement, so sudden tears. They can be talkative at different ages. As teenagers, though, they cannot listen and concentrate. They can be empathetic about friends and relatives and appear deeply involved. Yet they cannot remember where they're going or what lesson is next.

For those parents who suspect their daughter may have ADHD, the best place to begin is by calming down. The word "mental disorder" is scary, and many people tend to seek out symptoms in any action their child makes. This only serves to make everyone nervous. If your child behaves impulsively, it's not a confirmed diagnosis. Move past the impulse to make a judgment on every action.

Take your time. Don't judge by a single episode or even weekly behavior. ADHD is a constant disorder. So, if your daughter has it, it will show its consistency. Try watching your child's behavior throughout a month, making notes on the moments you consider abnormal.

Get an expert consultation. ADHD is a complex mental disorder. Sometimes it might only be a slight deviation from "normal" behavior. Sometimes even experienced specialists cannot establish it, and psychologists and neurologists are required.

Chapter 3: How I Knew that My Little Girl is Special

My daughter's name is Claire, and she's 15 years old now. She does very well in high school, but it wasn't always like that. In preschool, she was also academic, but primary school is where her grades failed dismally. Before going into her school years, let me speak about her early childhood.

I didn't realize something was different about my daughter in the beginning. She was born naturally, had a 9/9 Apgar score, and was healthy and calm. I breastfed her for up to 8 months, and we followed the doctor's advice in every respect, including vaccinations.

At three months old, Claire became whiny and started sleeping poorly. I would spend hours rocking her back and forth as she cried aloud. On the next visit to the doctor, I got a prescription for gas relief drops. We had additional tests, including an ultrasound of the brain. After the ultrasound, the doctor told me to visit the neurologist. That scared me a lot.

Subconsciously, I postponed the visit to the specialist. I was afraid my daughter had something diabolically wrong with her. However, I eventually went to the neurologist. The doctor said Claire was growing well and in line with her age. She performed several tests (like taking her by the hands and watching her hold her head, putting her on her stomach and watching her trying to crawl, etc.). All appeared OK, but the ultrasound results were suggested differently.

There were some abnormalities with the frontal lobe of her brain. The doctors mentioned it could be attributed to her increased anxiety and problems with sleeping. She said the issues should pass as she grew and that I should pay attention to any changes in her behavior. She prescribed exercises on the ball to develop fine motor skills with toys. She promoted some attachment parenting with skin on skin contact.

These recommendations helped, and Claire became more stable. Her sleep wasn't brilliant, but she improved and could sleep for an hour or two without waking up. Subsequently, her intensive crying became milder and not that frequent. However, it still happened, and she even started trembling during such attacks.

At 6 months, we took Claire for tests again, and she passed all tests and procedures. She slept for around five hours that day. Then suddenly, she woke up with a cry. I thought she was hungry and wanted a feed. It was clear she wasn't hungry. Instead, she threw back her head and cried aloud in bursts. Within minutes, she was trembling. Not just her hands and lower lip as before, but her whole body. I called the doctor, who said I should put her on the ball and rock back and forth and then try to feed her again. I tried this, and it worked, but just for a few minutes. That night was a nightmare.

These crying and trembling attacks continued. The neurologist said that possibly her brain deficiency was progressing and that we needed to have ultrasounds each month. In regards to her development, she was doing great. By almost seven months, she could sit on her own. Two weeks after that, she was able to crawl. I was elated by her success. By ten months, the trembling had almost disappeared too. But when she was desperate for a colorful toy, or when I spent too long in the bathroom, that horrible crying attack would begin. They were so intense, as though she couldn't breathe during them. She held her fists firmly and shook them around fast as though having a fit. Then she spread her fists apart, gasping for air, then started yelling. Calming her was difficult and tiresome.

There was no way of getting entirely rid of those attacks. Even by two years old, they were still there. The neurologist prescribed medication (a nootropic substance), resulting in an allergic reaction, so I couldn't test its efficiency. A substitute I tried had no effect. So I managed to organize my life so that there'd be no reason for Claire to get upset and have attacks. If she wasn't sleeping, I would always be with her. I allowed her to do as pleased unless it caused any harm. I kept dangerous things out of sight, such as electric cables, devices, gadgets, knives, scissors, and chemicals. It was inconvenient. Even using a blender meant unpacking, washing, drying, and putting away afterward. I was happy to do all of it, though, if it meant she wouldn't have an attack.

Cartoons were an efficient means to keep Claire occupied for an hour. I would read through forums in these times. I read that many other children did the same, which concerned me. She also behaved strangely after cartoons, moving in fast movements chaotically. She could exclaim the words she heard in the cartoon repeatedly. It wasn't typical of her, so I started looking for other ways to keep her occupied, so I could also get some chores done and look after myself.

I found an idea using interactive toys with various surfaces. I bought some toys and made the sample board myself. Then I cut pieces of cloth, plastic, paper, wood, metal, different shaped buttons and glued them to the board. It worked well. Claire liked to touch the pieces and spend a good twenty minutes at the board.

Another thing I learned over time is that my daughter needed a lot of motion. At the playground, she was one of the first to climb over a rope ladder, slide down the tube, get on the swings and then rock wildly. While I enjoyed being active and sporty, it was pretty challenging keeping her out of danger. If other children were rocking the swings, she wouldn't pay attention. She would go underneath, which always sent my heart into overdrive. She often ran very fast and would bump her head easily against a pillar or stairs. There was no way for me to stand still and chat as other moms and dads did. I always had to watch Claire and predict her next move to keep her—and other children—safe.

At 3 years, Claire was talking complete sentences, could assemble a 10-piece puzzle quickly, and was extremely fond of cats. Those aspects made me happy. But I still worried over her inability to not listen to me about dangers, or sitting and enjoying a moment, and not noticing other children. I told myself this was likely attributed to me, given I went out of my way so she wouldn't be upset. I knew I spoiled her but believed it would all settle down in time. So I made peace with it and stopped worrying.

Chapter 4: It is Very Important to Find the Right Doctor

Before I knew it, we were celebrating Claire's 5th birthday. That weekend we went to the park with Claire. I overheard a few other mothers talking about someone's nephew. She described the boy as unbearable, never listening, constantly shifting and running back and forth. Another mom sympathetically sighed and said, "Oh, those ADHD kids aren't easy to put up with."

When we got home that day, I researched the symptoms of ADHD. It was overwhelming. Some signs were similar to Claire's behavior but appeared to be unique to Claire. I sat there like I was shot. A mental disorder! It wasn't just a specific behavior but a mental illness! And it could stay with her throughout her life. There were different theories about the cause of ADHD, but official sites were saying it's likely genetics. What can I do against genetics? I felt reassured as I read further that children with ADHD can adapt to society and live capable lives. I needed to find some answers.

Get the Opinion of Several Experts

The next day, I made an appointment with the pediatrician. After examining Claire, he said her symptoms I described were pretty standard for children the same age with ADHD. He mentioned most experts didn't diagnose when it came to ADHD at five, as many signs were seen in healthy children. However, he was kind enough to issue a referral for the neurologist visit.

The neurologist repeated the same things that there wasn't a reason to suspect ADHD. It was too early to make any conclusions. She agreed, however, that many of Claire's behavioral patterns were similar to ADHD. She concluded that she felt optimistic that Claire would outgrow her difficulties and be OK. Their positivity made me feel mildly better, but my heart was still heavy with worry.

I admit, despite doctors, relatives, and friends telling me to relax and enjoy her childhood, I couldn't help but try to get to the bottom of it. I was adamant about the symptoms I saw in Claire. The way she looked at me, the way she moved; even her laugh was somewhat hysterical. I consoled myself by reading that my anxious fretting over her behavior was usual for parents. It was frustrating, with so much conflicting information. But I needed to help her, and staying optimistic was necessary.

Check the Doctor's Credentials

I learned about Dr. Chad Rhiny from the internet. He was a pediatric therapist in the neighboring town who offered diagnosis and adequate treatment. The more I researched about him, the safer I felt approaching him. He studied child psychiatry and was a reliable expert in the field. He was working on ADHD cases for his monograph.

Watch the Doctor's Attitude Towards the Child

I scheduled an appointment with Dr. Rhiny. When we arrived, he didn't examine Claire as I expected but allowed her to play in the playroom instead. He asked relentless questions over our lives for the past six years. How the pregnancy was, labor, how her first 12 months was, the following year, third, fourth, and so on. He kept watching Claire and once in a while would call her and show her something trivial like a pen, woven doll, or shiny stone. He didn't let her hold it and only wanted to gauge her reaction. At one interval, she tugged at the doll but then dropped it quickly and retreated to the playroom again. When he held up the stone, she raised her hand to touch it but didn't try to take it. She showed no interest in the pen.

I'm not sure how his tests were conducted and what he was looking for with his trials, but he concluded she was likely ADHD, combined type. He said he felt it was too early to know conclusively, and that went for therapy as well. However, he didn't feel that some symptoms were consistent or typical for ADHD. He compiled a list of rules Claire and I had to adhere to. These would hopefully strengthen her to interact better in social activities and academics. He said he wanted to see us again in six months.

At least this preliminary diagnosis allowed me to plan for the future. I felt this would be a big challenge, but one we could overcome.

Part II

Living with an ADHD Child

Chapter 5: How to Tell Your Daughter that She Needs Professional Help

The doctor suggested I be open with Claire about what was going on. I was reluctant to do this at first. But Claire continued to question everything. "Mommy, why should I wear protection when Laura (her friend) doesn't?" This was due to me buying knee and elbow protection due to all her accidents. Then she asked about her teacher. "My teacher likes to hold my hand when we go outside. She only holds my hand!" Claire believed the teacher thought she was unique, and that's why she chose her. But I suspected the truth was that the teacher was scared of Claire going down the stairs with the rest of the children and hurting herself. These actions made me wonder if I should open up to her.

Finally, I decided yes. Claire was a smart girl; she also had good empathy. I was at a loss, though, how to tell her. How do you explain a disorder to a 5-year old? What do you say? The more I thought about it, the more I understood I didn't have the words.

Plan Out What You Need to Say

Talking about a mental disorder might turn out to be stressful for your child. Pick the right words, accurate to their understanding and in a way that offers the most favorable outcome. I jotted down the main things I wanted Claire to know and how I should say them. I even wrote my "speech" in total. Then, I rehearsed it when I was alone. When we sat to talk, I changed things a lot, but this process definitely helped me in getting it all together in my head.

Select the Right Time

The best time to talk about something serious with your ADHD child is when he or she is physically and mentally relaxed. This might be after physical exercise or after a nap. You know your child best. When he or she isn't fidgeting and looks at you attentively, it's a good time. Likely, that frame of mind could change in ten minutes. So keep it brief and get to the point.

Pick Your Words

"Disorder", "problem", or "mental issue" aren't good words to tell your child. You may go into too much in explaining what those words mean, and they can sound scary. My chosen words were "you have different habits" and "think in another way". You could explain things like "brain works differently" for more grown-up kids. There's no sense in using the "ADHD" abbreviation when talking to a toddler, but you might say the word for a 10-year old. Just don't say, "You are/you've got ADHD." Better say, "That way of thinking/analyzing/behaving is called ADHD."

Be Optimistic but Not Careless

It's important to let your child realize ADHD isn't a disease and that it doesn't intervene with success in social life or studies. However, don't belittle it either. For example, I explained to Claire there was a chance that ADHD provoked her constantly losing toys and clothes. I told her it could all be overcome though and improved with exercises and, later, medication. Point out your child's strengths, such as running or being great at writing, so the conversation is still light and cheerful.

Reassure Your Child

Let your child understand that they aren't ill. There are simply challenges you need to tackle together. Try to involve them in working together on solutions. For example, "I know it's difficult for you to sit still and listen to a teacher. Let's think about what could help you do that? What if you have a softball you could squeeze in your hands, would that help?"

Explain Other People Might React Differently

I told Claire that the teacher was probably afraid of her falling on the stairs. That's why she held her by the hand on their trips outside and to the diner. We also talked about her impulsive behavior and sudden screams. It could happen during times of excitement or boredom. We played through the situation several times, changing roles, one of us screaming aloud when seeing something interesting. I explained it can be scary when someone screams and that the reason might not be apparent to other people. That's why they might react strangely. I suggested she express her excitement in other ways like, "I saw such a funny fly!" She liked this suggestion, and we did some role-playing for a while over different ways she could learn to express herself.

Being open with your child about ADHD helps in several ways:

1. Your child has a deeper understanding of what is going on.

2. Together, you can develop strategies and tactics.

3. They're more open to specific exercises and training skills.

4. It builds trust.

5. It justifies ongoing visits to the doctor and taking medication.

I found telling Claire that it didn't change things; it only made her pay closer attention, so she wasn't so easily distracted. In that way, she didn't feel like there was something "wrong" with her. Your child needs to understand that if they talk to you about their problems, they have your support at all times.

Chapter 6: Developing New Habits Together

Using Toys as a Way of Teaching

The therapist gave a lot of advice for me as the mother too. It made me understand that specific behavior patterns can be provoked by ADHD and weren't necessarily a whim or Claire being manipulative. For example, running head over heels and bumping into anything in her way (like a swing). I shouldn't have scolded her for such behavior. I should have expressed the dangers of such actions instead. I developed the following routine:

- Name the danger. This strategy was about her learning to be aware of her environment. "It's metal and heavy" or "it can bump and hurt".

- Demonstrate the process. Using the swing as an example, I'd swing it softly so it touched her, and she could feel its action.

- Say what to do. I told Claire she needed to say what she needed to do to avoid danger. "Make a circle around the swing when I'm running."

- Show what to do. I drew a large circle with the chalk around the swing.

- Fix the impression/skill with the story or a tale and go through the routine together.

I used her favorite fluffy bunny in the story. "Once, there was a bunny who went under the swing while a big frog was sitting on it. The bunny thought it would be fun. But the frog then did a big kick with its back legs and hit the bunny's ears. The bunny got scared as the wind seemed to roar in its ears. It lay flat on the ground (in this way, I described what to do if Claire happened to get in such a predicament) and waited until the frog stopped kicking its legs. Luckily, the frog noticed the bunny and stopped. After that, the bunny was always looking out for the swing when it was playing."

Utilize Stickers for Danger

To let Claire remember about the danger of some things (like knives, electric devices, an oven, etc.), I put different colored stickers on them. When she was small, it was mainly the color that attracted her attention. But at 6 years, she could read the stickers and write them herself. For example, she put a red sticker on her glue stick with the words "close me". She often left it open before the sticker. Once, the glue poured all over the papers, scissors, and other things in her box. There was a blue sticker on the door of our fridge, also instructing her to close it. Her water bottle also had a pink sticker saying "fill me" to fill it before going out to her sports activities.

Games, Activities, and Tasks

Another recommendation I got was to establish a daily routine and adhere to it diligently. It had nothing to do with sleep or eating habits but activities. My task was to make a daily schedule.

- Have active and passive tasks. Active could be doing sports or playing in the playground. Passive could be making sandcastles or reading a book.

- Alternate the tasks. Active, then passive, then active again.

- Start with 5-minute time slots for the passive tasks. Active ones can be allocated up to half an hour.

- Progressively add more time to passive activities. Work your way from five up to ten minutes.

- Prolong the inactive time by changing to different tasks. Perhaps after a sandcastle is made, read a book. Try to get them to stay in one place the whole time.

Illustrate Rules and Mutually Agree on Them

Together, we made a board where we agreed on the rules. Each rule was written with one word only along with a picture. Claire drew all the pictures. For example, "Conversation" was illustrated by a cup.

This rule taught Claire to wait rather than interrupt people when talking. I suggested she imagine everyone talking had a cup of tea. When she was overwhelmed with needing to speak in that second, she needed to pretend we wanted a sip of our tea first. It forced her to focus on waiting just a few seconds longer. After a month of doing this, Claire's teacher told me that her attention to stories was definitely improving.

Though these new habits required effort, both physical and mental, I noticed positive changes. Claire and I became more organized. Her impulsive actions and yelling didn't disappear but became less frequent. She started expressing herself differently, using more words instead like "I'm surprised" or "That's funny".

Chapter 7: Organizing Space at Home

When Claire started walking, there was no area in the home she wasn't active. Until she was 9, Claire emptied entire drawers to find one thing, even if it was on top. Her toys would be scattered everywhere, often breaking them. When painting or drawing something with marker pens, she bunched them all together instead of using one thing at a time. Those brushes and pens ended up in unlikely spots like a shoe or a flower pot afterward.

Indoor Sport Stands

Having a sports stand at home helped me enormously during the rainy days when there was no possibility to go outside. Claire liked climbing over a rope ladder, going through a mini-labyrinth, and swinging on a rope. When she grew older, she asked me to purchase a yoga mat for exercises. The monkey bars were also installed permanently in her room, and she could train herself doing simple exercises:

- Climbing

- Rope climbing

- Hanging and straightening her spine

- Push-ups

- Turnovers

- Cleaning

Decluttering and tidying Claire's room I did myself in the early days. It was an effort as for every one thing I picked up, she dropped another two. With the help of her therapist, I learned to turn this into a positive outcome. We often played together with her toys. Stumbling over them, I had become used to it. So I tried to make tidying up something fun. I placed a box in every room. We had to go into each room, find all the toys, and put them in the box. When distracted, I handed her tongs to entice her to continue and she enjoyed picking up toys with them.

When Claire was about seven years old, I gave her the task of sorting gathered articles. She also enjoyed vacuuming. After the cleaning, we made tea (see the section about fragile objects). We enjoyed drinking it and eating Claire's favorite donuts. We didn't suddenly have a clutter-free home, but it improved. Even at 15, the house is cluttered with her belongings. But she can now at least tidy up without my help. And we still drink tea with donuts together afterward.

Fragile Objects

I cannot count the times I removed broken cups, dishes, vases, and other fragile things from the table or floor. When Claire was running inside the house, tables, dish racks, cupboards, you name it, would be knocked. I learned to avoid wall-standing lamps in the interior and fitted the cupboard shutters with latches.

To help Claire be attentive when she was near the breakable objects, we developed a game. Claire used to point at random things such as a jar, crystal ball, or a chair, and I had to name the object. After that, we discussed what is and isn't breakable. The rule was, "first look, then touch". Claire had to look at the object she intended to touch or take first. It worked, though there were many times she forgot to apply the rule and had to catch the falling cup or look at the fragments on the floor. I told her she was doing well in those situations, then we cleaned up and bought a new one together.

Stress Release

While Claire gradually succeeded in paying closer attention and controlling herself, there were times when she became restless and nervous. We went outside, and Claire rode her bike or roller skates in those times. It helped release her inner tension. If she didn't have that outlet, she was prone to sudden outbursts of anger or irritation. When there was no option to go outside, I told Claire to go to her room and shout into her pillow. For that, I bought several big pillows without pictures. She used to scream into the pillow, crumple it in her hands, and then throw it onto the floor. After that, she became calmer and more composed.

Studying

When Claire got sick with a cold, I tried to do the preschool tasks with her. We used to paint, color, mold clay, and learn the numbers together. While she was usually involved in the task, she easily got distracted. Her pens and pencils ended up all over the place too. To solve that problem, we agreed on gathering all pencils into the left drawer of Claire's desk and pens into the right one. I switched off the TV in the hall and shut the windows so that there'd be no distracting sounds. Sometimes, I used to turn on quiet and relaxing music. Now, at 15, Claire has a separate playlist for her studies. It's predominantly instrumental focus tunes. She puts her headphones on and completes her homework. She also tidies up her table before starting to write. And there's still a separate drawer for pencils.

At first, I tried to set a timer for Claire, so she knew when to take time out and relax and not be overwhelmed with homework. However, it turned out the timer became a stress factor for her. She paid too much attention to when it would go off and instead rush through her work to get it done before it beeped. So we came up with another routine instead. When

Claire felt as though she was dizzy and needed time out, she could occupy herself with any other task she wanted to. It could be reading a book or trying her clothes on.

Organizing the space for your ADHD child might be tiresome, and you might be at a loss where to start. However, once you establish achievable goals and routines, it's reachable. In our case, some things made the process smoother:

- Be positive, even if you're not successful at first.

- Encourage your child and praise them when they've done well.

- Explain to them the meaning of each rule you establish and how it should help.

- Be attentive, and let them manage their private space on their own. Over time, they'll learn to be more organized.

Part III

School Life

Chapter 8: The Preschool Years

When Claire was 5, I felt reluctant to send her to preschool. She bumped her head several times every day and would never listen to anyone for more than two minutes at that stage or obey any rules. I was so scared something horrible would happen to her or other children. More than once, I had to prevent her from jumping off swings or throwing heavy toys at random in excitement.

Don't Blame Yourself for a Separation

When she was at school, I finally found some time for myself. It felt like a blessing after all the years of constant alert. I could go where I wished and do what I wanted. If you have someone to help you with your child, I recommend not waiting for 5 years to some time out for yourself now and then. Don't be afraid to look selfish. A confident, healthy mother is a crucial factor in the child's confidence level. As I managed to rest, both physically and mentally, Claire began to change too. She became more composed and started to talk in a more articulated way and talk and play with other kids. However, her fast and abrupt movements remained, along with constantly hurting herself and bumping into things. Her knees, palms, and elbows were bruised continuously and scratched.

Imitate the Preschool Routine

I researched a lot when I prepared Claire for preschool. I made an effort to adjust her routine to mimic what she would experience at school. We role-played being "a child" and "a teacher". We watched cartoons and educational videos for toddlers going to preschool. I went to the preschool beforehand without Claire, which I felt was a good decision. She would have noticed how insecure I was feeling otherwise. Looking around the classrooms and play areas made me feel safe that everything would be OK. Once speaking to the teacher, she put me at utter ease. When I told her about Claire, she didn't seem surprised. She said such behavior was typical for many kids her age and that she'll take care of her and that everything would be fine. She suggested I stay with Claire for her first few days at preschool.

Discuss Problems with Teachers Openly

To my surprise (and joy), she felt good at preschool. I read so much about separation anxiety during these times, so I felt happy she was enjoying it. On the first day, she released my hand and ran to the toys on the floor. She took a miniature train and started pushing it back and forth. By the third day, it was evident I could leave her there without fear. I was open with her teacher about her episodes. She queried if there was any medication she should be taking, of which there wasn't. The teacher frowned a bit but nevertheless smiled at me and said there was a doctor and that everything would be fine.

Learning to Keep Focused

Another thing that bothered me was her inability to listen to others. While she was attentive to the preschool teacher, she didn't always hear what was going on. She also ran off somewhere or started doing things that hadn't been agreed upon. For example, the teacher could start saying, "Now, we're going to color in the fox." While the other children were still listening to the rest of the instructions, Claire was already storming ahead and taking everything out to begin.

Claire would sit still for tasks such as cutting paper or painting. However, when the teacher read a book, Claire would not sit on the mat for long with the other kids. She stood up and wandered around, picked up toys, looked into the bathroom and distracted herself doing other things. When the teacher asked her about the tale afterward, she could answer some questions.

To help Claire focus on the story, the teacher would allow her to sit on a fitness ball while listening so she could rock herself back and forth. She also introduced putting her hands into bowls full of beads or buttons to stimulate herself in other ways while the story was being read. When I found out about it, I made my own bowl at home for Claire. This bowl is still in her room, and she likes to go through the objects when she needs relaxation.

Learning Patience

What was difficult for her at school was keeping her turn. If they were doing an exercise where everyone had to wait their turn, she wouldn't understand that she had to wait. With some of the other kids, it would lead to an argument. Explanations didn't help. The teacher needed to remind Claire at that moment that she had to wait, and then she would do so. Reminders, though, were essential.

Her education continued successfully. She quickly learned her letters and numbers. The teacher said her memory sequence was good, and she was always among the first students to remember a new song or dance. It took her longer, though, to understand how letters could be formed together. Eventually, she got there, and it was a pure joy both for her and myself. By the time Claire went to elementary school, she could read a short story and write her name and simple one-syllable words.

Chapter 9: Elementary School

Dealing with Complex Tasks

Moving to elementary school, the increase in subjects and projects became difficult for Claire. She struggled to do homework for three different topics in a row. When I checked her books, her writing was more irregular than previously and more mistakes than usual. Letters within each word were obsolete. Instead of writing the word "dolly", she'd just write "dl." Or, at times, she wrote it correctly but then wrote it twice.

What helped was splitting the tasks so that Claire could do one subject at a time. If there was a lot to do, she made sure to take a break between each task. In each break, we talked or had a drink and assembled some puzzles so she could de-stress herself.

Concealing Lower Grades

Claire continued to attend school, and we often discussed how school was going when she was home. However, she was reluctant when talking about any marks connected with her schoolwork. On any other topic, Claire could ramble on endlessly. She took half an hour describing how it eventually started raining and that under umbrellas, they listened to drops falling. Getting her to open up about different classes and what stories they were reading at school was another issue. I pushed, and this caused her to clam up even more. She started avoiding our conversations about school and would sit in her room instead for hours.

After consulting with the therapist, I adopted a temporary "no question" rule. I would have general conversations with Claire but didn't bring up school work. She was suspicious about this initially but soon relaxed. In a short time frame, she began to feel as though she could open up about school again.

Nail Biting

When Claire started school, her usual nail-biting intensified. Her nails were no longer the only areas she bit, and her teeth would nibble on the skin, which sometimes drew blood. Her mannerisms were chaotic again, and her nervous tension was evident.

The therapist suggested avoiding additional stress, positive and negative, and simplifying things for a while. I needed to make sure that her life was stable and not too complicated. This meant I had to cancel a new theatre study she was about to attend. She was disappointed about that.

Within a month, though, this helped. Claire was using nail clippers to cut her nails, and she was biting them less. It was a positive sign. Her impulsive behavior calmed down again too.

Discuss Problems and Solutions with Teachers

When I approached the teacher, Mr. Johns, he told me that Claire did well in her studies but lacked attention to detail. He didn't seem to notice her hyperactivity in class. After the therapist's consultation, I talked to Mr. Johns again and told him about Claire's diagnosis. He appeared surprised but listened attentively. He was glad I confided in him as it made him understand her academic behavior more. We discussed her school work in detail and concluded a few agreements regarding relaxing punishment in specific cases. It might be searching for a pen for a large part of a lesson, or not finishing a math task, or forgetting where the diner was.

The teacher's attitude is profoundly important, and I advise you to leave behind all concerns and talk directly. After all, the teacher is the person your child will spend a lot of time with, so it's essential everyone is informed and comfortable.

We also came to an agreement on suitable punishments. If Mr. Johns was telling a child, they needed to take time out and sit on a chair, this wasn't going to work for Claire as she wouldn't stay seated.

So we agreed that penalties could be missing out on a group game or missing her turn for something.

Losing Objects

There wasn't much academic progress despite talking to the teacher. Often the space where her homework should be written was blank, and I had to message the teacher to get it. Claire continued to forget things like pens, markers, training shoes, lunch boxes, and even her backpack often. However, she was doing well overall, and her nail-biting was almost non-existent. If any challenge arose, though, such as a test, or gym competition, she bit her nails again.

The solution during this stage was always having a backup. Claire had a box in her locker that contained additional stationery. The locker even had an extra pair of school pants, shirt, and sneakers. Once a week, I went to the school to replenish any missing items.

Limiting TV and Gadgets

The therapist recommended I adhered to limited time spent watching television. I allowed her to watch television or YouTube on my phone for a maximum of half an hour daily. At the beginning of elementary school, Claire would spend two hours or more watching television, so this was a significant deduction. When the time was lessened, I noticed a considerable improvement in her schoolwork and general attitude.

She became more attentive and overreacted to the teacher's remarks or another child's less often. Until the end of elementary school, she averaged around B+ to A. She was still impulsive and would forget things. She was definitely less chaotic, and she could do three-step math tasks with little effort. There were still times she missed letters, but her writing was comprehensive in general.

Chapter 10. Middle School

Continue with Activities

When middle school began, Claire was much more organized and attentive than she used to be. She attended dance classes for a year, and it did her good in releasing muscle tension. We tried multiple hand-made clubs such as knitting, molding, paper cutting, and origami. This helped with relieving mental stress. She expressed enjoying puzzles, so I bought some for her, and she spent over an hour concentrating on them.

Less Parental Control

I stopped checking her school books and only looked through the homework diary once a week. I also only checked the teachers' reports when they were available. She did a lot better in the classes where she liked the teachers. She still had "B+" grades. And teachers often remarked that her knowledge in specific areas deserved an A. It was often careless mistakes that led to the lower grade. For example, she made a brilliant representation for a history class but forgot to mention any dates.

Balance Social Life and Studies

As she approached her teens, Claire became more secretive. She didn't share much of her school life and thoughts with me, but she chatted endlessly with her friends. Claire would be easily irritated when I followed up if she had her scarf or pocket money. She objected fiercely when I told her I would go to school and talk with her teachers about her disorder. She didn't want anyone to know. She said she did well in her studies, so what more did I want?

By the end of her first year in middle school, I noticed her grades had lowered. When I asked her about it, she was visibly upset but had no intention of confiding in me. Perhaps having a phone and endless chats with friends were the problem. Often when I entered her room, she put the phone under a book or next to the computer and pretended to be busy with her studies. When I called her teachers, almost all of them told me she was inattentive during lessons and seldom willing to answer questions.

I needed Claire to manage her time properly. I understood social media was typical at that age, but I couldn't let it interfere with her studies and grades at school.

Accept Professional Help

I suggested to Claire to go to the therapist again. To my surprise, she agreed. We made an appointment, but this time everything was different.

Although he addressed most of his questions to Claire, Dr. Rhiny invited us both into his room. He didn't question her about school. He asked about her future aspirations, what she enjoyed in her life and if she enjoyed social media, and so on.

When Claire relaxed, Dr. Rhiny explained she could relay any trouble she deemed necessary, and we could figure out solutions together. Claire's eyes got teary at that point, and I reached over to take her by the hand.

She then confessed she found it so hard to keep her attention on something. It was as though everything was happening around her at speeds she struggled to cope with. She said there'd been a fallout with her best friend Leyla when she forgot her birthday. Claire started crying, and that was heartbreaking for me.

The therapist waited until Claire had calmed down. He then explained that these were pretty typical things in a teenager's life, regardless of ADHD. She felt encouraged by those words.

Dr. Rhiny suggested different ways of dealing with Claire's memory gaps and inability to concentrate on a task. One way was organizing her time and environment. Another was to take medication. He said it wasn't "mind changing" but could help Claire concentrate, at least in the short term. He warned about possible side effects and said the dosage shouldn't be increased beyond the prescribed amount. It was amphetamine, and Claire needed to take it daily.

Adhere Strictly to Prescription Doses

To my surprise, Claire agreed to both of the doctor's suggestions. Within three days, she mentioned feeling more focused. Her essay on Africa's wildlife received the highest grade. She also didn't lose any of her fancy keychains that week either. The dance contest a week later, she nailed beautifully.

At one point, she had a very challenging day ahead. Claire asked if she could take another pill in the evening as she needed to finish her IT task and couldn't concentrate on it. It was too late to call the therapist, so I advised her to sleep and finish her homework the following day.

When I called Dr. Rhiny, he stressed that Claire shouldn't increase the dosage by any means. Taking more medication wouldn't help overcome the ADHD symptoms. It could, though, develop side effects. Sticking to the recommended dose would allow her to remain focused.

Make Notes

On the organizational part, Claire and I did well. I made her a gift—a lovely dairy, where she put down her plans and appointments. The diary had a shoulder strap, and Claire took it everywhere. She wrote down all her tasks, and together we went through the schedule. We put together a time-management plan for her studies, rehearsals, and activities. This helped, and she felt more confident about what she needed to get done. She also put all her friends' birthdays (and mine) into the diary.

Family Can Help

The hardest part was abandoning her phone during the time allotted for studying. We agreed that I would take Claire's phone while doing her homework. I was tempted to break the rule when she came to me 15 minutes later asking for it. I let her have it at that time. However, next time Claire didn't ask for the phone, and we celebrated this small victory after the homework was finished.

Our time management involved household tasks as well. We agreed in advance when cleaning or cooking needed doing. Claire would write it in her planner and always kept her word. She was still impulsive at times. If the cleaning took longer than usual, she threw the vacuum or left the dishes unwiped on the table. I learned not to do the work for her. Once she had a few moments of making peace with herself, she came back to finish the task. She was more organized, and her grades increased. She was at a stage where receiving an A was standard, and she'd be disappointed with a B+.

Part IV
Social Life

Chapter 11. How We Learned to Develop Emotions

Children with ADHD are often buoyant and noisy (except those with only the attention deficit type). Claire still was to some extent as well. Sometimes she could be intense and dramatic, and you couldn't always get the desired results. I also didn't always want to point out, though, that ADHD might be the issue. For example, I could sit with Claire for an hour explaining to her the anatomy of the human heart and blood vessels. She'd understand perfectly. But within ten minutes, she may not remember any of it.

I found it difficult not to get angry or irritated in these moments. If Claire saw I was mad, she would become angry too. So, it was a two-way venture in keeping our emotions in check.

Keep Control of Emotions

Getting angry with your child never helps. If your child has little interest in a task, anger will only decrease their interest in it. If your child is trying to remember, don't scold them; otherwise, they'll simply stop trying.

Even as teenagers, our children need to depend on us emotionally. It might require a lot of effort to stay calm and look for a constructive solution. Listen to your teenager and show them that working through emotions is how we overcome them.

Be Open About Feelings

While you don't want to shout at your child, showing emotions isn't a bad thing. We're not robots, and we have emotions and feelings too, and we're allowed to express ourselves. In doing so, our children see that emotions are natural, and so is working through them. For example, when Claire broke another expensive television when she hit it with her dancing ball, I didn't scold her. But I raised my voice considerably when it happened and was very upset.

I explained that we had fewer cinema nights to save for a new one. Being open doesn't always work with a teenager. Sometimes, Claire just didn't hear me at all. However, when she saw I was upset, she usually asked what happened.

Name the Emotion

For a child, emotions are fundamental. For Claire, they were at times overwhelming, making her scream at the top of her voice. I learned that naming emotions and describing her state helped Claire. When she couldn't remember a song's lyrics for the school choir, I told her feeling frustrated was normal.

It often helped. Knowing what she was feeling was normal, allowed her to work through problems.

I did the same with positive emotions. If Claire saw a puppy on the street and exclaims loudly with joy, I assisted by talking through feelings. "What a lovely puppy, right? What a joy! And he's so cute I want to hug him."

Be Supportive

Always consider your child's ADHD. Once when Claire was 13, she hit a boy with her backpack for no apparent reason. I was next to her at the time. I apologized to the boy and told her we'd discuss it at home. When at home, Claire was in tears. She said the boy was bullying her, and she couldn't help it, she retaliated. While I presumed Claire wasn't telling me everything, I left it at that. I offered to help make peace with him but Claire said she'd do it herself. She promised not to hit anyone. I learned that prying too much wouldn't help either of us—some things she needed to sort out herself. However, showing support at all times was essential.

Chapter 12. The Social Problems We Faced and Overcame

Not Girlish Behavior

Claire had a nickname of "free spirit" among the parents' community at a local playground from a young age. I never considered it negative. Other girls were calmer and could spend more time sitting or standing in one place than Claire. On the other hand, Claire looked active and daring at all times. She challenged every element the playground offered. Over time, I acknowledged she was generally alone. Other girls groped at four years old, talking and doing things together. Claire never participated and ran around alone or with the boys.

I didn't regard this as a problem initially, as I thought it was Claire's character—active and independent. Still, now I understand that ADHD partly caused her inability to sit still and play quietly. Her behavior changed over time as she grew.

Too Impulsive

When Claire started to pay attention to other girls and boys and tried to make friends, she was often rejected. Some accepted her friendship and ran with her. When the game changed, Claire was left running on her own. When she did sit and build sandcastles, she waved her arms widely and exclaimed her excitement. When that happened, sand would spray in other kid's faces, and they'd cry or yell at Claire. I would remove her from the situation and tell her it wasn't the way to act.

During the teenage period, Claire's outbursts sometimes got her in trouble. She exclaimed loudly during a movie they were watching. It was difficult for her not to talk aloud during classes. She understood these outbursts did her no good, but she struggled to control them. A psychology course about emotional control helped her considerably. The impulsiveness stayed with her but became less intense and troublesome.

Breaking the Rules

An ADHD child often breaks the rules at home, school, and on the playground. It isn't the result of "poor behavior" but rather a symptom of the nervous system being overexcited. Don't tell your child what he or she shouldn't do. It works better if you say what they should do. For example, saying, "Don't throw the sand onto other children." or "Stop playing games on the phone." won't work. Change it around and instead say, "Let's play Captain America and save other children from this nasty sand."

When Claire didn't want to part with her phone in her teenage years and do her homework, I asked her to help me water the flowers or do my hair. Distractions worked well, and she could then quickly shift her attention rather than being faced with a negative.

When Claire hit her teens, she started overreacting to many of my suggestions, no matter how I tried to express them. I learned to get straight to the point and talk openly. I also explained why I wanted something from her and my emotions. If I wanted Claire to do her homework, I said something like, "Please get to your biology. I'm worried there won't be enough time for it in the evening." It often worked, and though Claire seldom changed her mind, she didn't slam doors or shout aloud.

Blurred Privacy

During the preschool period, if Claire wanted to run around and slide down the playground, there was no use persuading her otherwise. Claire often grabbed children by the hand and onto the swings with her. She didn't understand privacy and snatched other children's toys and thought nothing of it. I tried to persuade her to give it back and that she didn't have permission to take it.

If that didn't work, I had to unclench it from her hands and return it. She then started crying hysterically. I always remained firm in those moments, and her tears would cease quickly.

Afterward, I would talk to her. We played a doll theatre and re-enact the situation of "aggressors" and "victims". It helped gradually. At 5, Claire started asking before taking someone's toy and children were more willing to play with her.

This problem was partly present during her teens too. Acting under impulse or being inattentive, Claire sometimes took other students' stationery and even phones. At first, she wasn't willing to admit that she had something that didn't belong to her. If it was a small item, such as a keychain or hairband, she'd feel scared to give it back to the owner. She often tried to return the things secretly, which sometimes caused suspicions with other children.

Talking with Claire and persuading her to approach the owner directly often failed. She didn't want to admit that she took something. The psychologist I spoke to recommended a therapy course to increase self-confidence and training of personal boundaries. I attended the classes with Claire, and it helped us both. Claire became less nervous, and, when taking someone else's things, she apologized and returned them. It also improved classroom relationships, which in turn enhanced her self-esteem.

Not Too Social

To let Claire socialize in her early years, I introduced games that would be active. When we were going to a playground, we used to take relay race cones, a ball, and a jump rope. I tried to make the games interactive for all so that Claire could learn to act socially with others. We used to play tangling knots with the jump rope, or hot potato, or a relay race with small awards like candy. Later on, when Claire invited friends over from school, it was vital to entertain her friends.

When Claire reached her teens, she was pleasant. However, some minor ADHD symptoms still caused some stressful episodes with her friends. Once, her girlfriend Amanda called, and Claire refused to talk to her. She sat sulkily and wasn't willing to do anything. Finally, she said that Amanda had come up with a nickname for her, "a lost bunny", and some children liked it and started calling her that. The name was due to Claire losing things all the time and forgetting where she'd placed items.

I learned not to be presumptuous about a situation. I listened and expressed my feelings when Claire wanted me to. I felt sorry for her as I knew the problem was unpleasant. To my surprise, Claire asked if she was acting like a lost bunny. I had to pick my words tactfully so as not to offend her, but at the same time remind her that she did lose things frequently. Claire smiled then and admitted there was a logical reason for the nickname. Following the psychologist's advice, we learned through courses, Claire drew a picture of herself looking like a bunny with a broad smile. We both laughed at the image, and Claire felt much better. The next call from Amanda, she answered and made peace. Her social skills improved, and she felt good spending time with her friends.

Chapter 13. Living with an ADHD Teenage Girl

Everything changes so fast as children grow up. Before you know it, they've worked their way around the school, peers, and social surroundings. But not willing to listen to advice throughout it all, I realized this fact was simply Claire being herself. The good news, this is normal. The not-so-good news is that you'll need to put in a lot of effort.

Revise the Rules

Claire used to clean her room up until she was 10. I can't say that it was a great clean, but a clean. As a teenager, she abandoned cleaning altogether. Talking and threatening to take away her devices didn't work either. So I had to come up with another way. On the weekend, I asked her about cleaning and doing other household tasks. She replied that she didn't have time. I replied that I would happily take over her duties. However, it would mean I had no time for cooking or ironing then. She stopped to think about that. Reluctantly, she then agreed she would clean her room. Claire would then vacuum all the rooms as I dusted. She liked cleaning after looking at the rules from a different angle.

Accept and Support

As a teenager, natural hormonal changes are happening. ADHD symptoms on top of those hormones, such as poor concentration, inability to plan, and impulsive behavior, become even more present. There's no way but to accept these changes and offer your support. A therapist's advice can help immensely. If your child decides to confide in you, be ready to listen without judgment. Ask if they need your advice, as perhaps they just need an ear to listen.

Don't Attribute Everything to ADHD

"Justifying" the poor grade or unsocial behavior with the disorder can be risky. A teenager might accept this as a method of psychological protection and stop trying, knowing they have an escape route. "It's the disorder," Claire said once when she failed to get a place in a dancing contest. I told her firmly that it wasn't true. I reminded her she often won contests and that in this one, she didn't rehearse much. I let her make that conclusion herself.

Ensure Stability

Stress can easily be multiplied for a child with ADHD if external circumstances are unstable. We planned to move to another city when Claire was 13. We discussed it with her, and she seemed excited about it. However, afterward, her poor concentration and fidgeting symptoms renewed. Having consulted with the therapist, we postponed the resettlement. The symptoms got weaker in a few weeks, and Claire went back to normal.

Be Flexible

At times logically talking with Claire had its difficulties. She could be very stubborn to the point where she'd withdraw mentally and physically. There were times I held firm in my position (like not buying a new phone three months after the previous one), and times were explaining things was best. I tried to find another way out. For example, I was making a joke about decorating the New Year tree with Claire's phones.

Stay Positive

Don't indulge in your emotions by criticizing your child no matter how bitter you may feel. It's good to explain your point and end with some encouragement briefly. Once Claire smashed the bulb on the demonstration stand in the school laboratory by turning abruptly and hitting it with her backpack. We talked about the matter. Claire insisted there was no way of passing it without touching it. I objected and said if she had moved with less haste, she would have touched it but not smashed it. I told her then that she was faster than everyone else, of which we then both laughed.

There are many other ways of dealing with teenagers with ADHD. Much of the practical advice can also be used for all teenagers. I tried to describe what happened with my daughter having a combined ADHD type.

Epilogue

This story is a personal one about my daughter Claire. I've tried to relay the problems we encountered due to having ADHD. You may find that you might discover there are not many typical ADHD symptoms by reading through this book. But ADHD is a disorder that can be more or less expressed in many different forms. Claire has the combined form, although she didn't show any "hyper" behavior or a complete lack of concentration. If it weren't for Dr. Rhiny, the therapist, I'd still be feeling lost. Getting professional advice helps more than you can imagine.

I'm sure there's no universal guide for ADHD. The symptoms vary due to individual attitudes, environment, and social relationships. Some children do better with medication, and some don't. Some make use of the anti-stress toys, and others detest them. Some children learn basic skills like reading and writing quickly but have poor grades.

I wanted to show that ADHD isn't a sentence through this book. There's no complete cure of symptoms, and they may stay with your child throughout their life. But life is colorful, and there are many ways to teach your child to cope. There's no one-size-fits-all. Claire enjoys making notes in her planner and taking on short-term projects. Another teenager might have other methods and tools. I encourage you, though, as the parent, to try various methods to find your way of dealing with ADHD.

Another thing I would like to point out is that you shouldn't make decisions on behalf of your child. Teenagers, in general, don't like it, and a teenager with ADHD might react very negatively to it.

Claire and I have lived with and dealt with ADHD for 15 years. She's lively and social; she has friends, loves chatting, history, and geography. Claire takes prescribed medications, but the doctor gives them when she direly needs them. She's still forgetful and often leaves things at friend's houses. However, by the time she's home, she will have remembered where she left it. She doesn't fidget anymore, and she rarely bites her nails with excitement or disappointment.

Not too far ahead, she will be an adult. It'll have its challenges and new conditions to adapt to. I'm sure my daughter will figure it all out as she progresses. And she knows I'm always there to support her.

Printed in Great Britain
by Amazon

14054286R00047